SELF-EMPLOYED AND LOVING IT!

How To Be Happy Working For Yourself

Rodger Cornell

DEDICATION

I would like to dedicate this book to my wife and children, who inspired and assisted me throughout the book's development.

To my daughter Alicia for the formatting.

To my brother, Philip (the old curmudgeon), for the editing.

To Sean Taylor and Jeff Pera for the cover work.

TABLE OF CONTENTS

CHAPTER 1: YOU'RE UP, YOU'RE DOWN

The phone was ringing. I rolled over to check the alarm clock. It showed 3:20 a.m. and I knew, before my wife Eileen picked up the phone on her night table, that it was the cops. They were calling to tell us that the alarm at our restaurant had gone off.

As I drove the four miles from our home to the Pump House, I thought FIVE! This was the fifth time in the four years since we had the alarm system installed that I'd driven these early morning, empty streets half asleep (and once half in the bag).It was a big inconvenience. It was also worth the inconvenience. In the ten years prior to the alarm being installed we'd been broken into half a dozen times, with the same results: A window was broken, food and liquor taken, the register forced open and damaged. A couple of times some random vandalism was tossed in. Even though money was never taken (we never left any overnight), there was a considerable dollar- value loss from the items stolen and damage to the building. There was also a residual, very unpleasant feeling of vulnerability and violation.

I pulled into the restaurant parking lot and was approached by a Mount Olive Township police sergeant and two patrolmen. I knew the sergeant from past break-ins. Yelling to be heard over the wailing alarm, he informed me that it didn't look as though any one had broken in, so would I please unlock the door and turn off the goddamn alarm before any more of my neighbors went ballistic (there had already been three, very irate calls to the dispatcher).

I unlocked the kitchen door, and pushing past me, flashlight in hand, and service revolver drawn, the sergeant entered the building. At his ok I followed, flicking on the light switch just inside the door. I instantly knew that something was very wrong. My first thought was fire! The kitchen was filled with smoke, but the "smoke" didn't swirl and billow, it just hung there like fog or, more accurately, like one of those globes that you shake to create a snow storm over a miniature village. Here, however, the snowflakes were gray. A glance to my right solved the mystery; the entire cooking line was covered with about a half inch of this snow. Ranges, griddle, salamander broiler, ovens and fat fryer were coated with the stuff. The Ansel fire suppression system had gone off!

An Ansel system consists of several metal pipes, capped with plastic, that hang over the cooking surfaces. These pipes all lead to a large canister filled with powder. In the event of a fire on any of the cooking surfaces the heat melts the plastic cap, the powder is released and the flames are smothered. The released powder had triggered the motion detectors and set of the alarm! It was the pipe over the fat fryer that had released, and judging by the blackened wall behind the fryer, and a melted "220" wall socket, it had done its' job and extinguished a grease fire. That fryer was a big electric unit that, according to a regular customer, who was a union electrician, drew more amps the most homes. It was an older model that lacked a high temperature cut off, and on several occasions had to be quickly turned off because it gone over 500 degrees and was incinerating whatever was in it at the time. Of course, the fryer was turned off at the end of the night right? Wrong! This was my night off and obviously the crew that closed up had left this monster on.

I turned off the alarm and explained what had happened to the sergeant, who wished me luck and left. Cursing Luis, the kitchen crew chief, I phoned my wife and described the mess facing us. She called a friend -a very good friend- to come and watch our four kids. Eileen arrived at the restaurant within an hour. Meanwhile, I had located an electrician who was willing to come out at that hour to repair the circuit damage, enticed with a promise of fast payment and all our future business.

While he worked to restore power to the line, Eileen and I surveyed the damage. The "snow" covering the charred fat fryer was the least of it. The opening between our kitchen and the "front of the house" had no door so every surface and I mean every square inch of every surface, in the kitchen, in the bar and in the dining room, was coated with powder. Worse, we found that this stuff was greasy and hard to remove. Hercules in the stables had nothing on us!

At 7a.m. we began to call in employees, Luis got the first call and Barbara, the waitress who locked up, got the second. By 9a.m. we had nine people cleaning. Besides cleaning all the surfaces including walls, floors, and ceilings several times, anything that would come in contact with food (dishes, pots, pans, utensils) had to be run through the dishwasher. Cloth surfaces (drapes, carpet, linens) had to be vacuumed, or taken to the Laundromat. Anything made of paper (lunch napkins, menus, placemats, and more) had to be tossed.

We opened for business at 4p.m., twelve hours after the sergeant and I first walked in the kitchen. We did 26 dinners and some bar business that night, which didn't begin to cover the cost of the electrician, employees and cleaning materials. Eileen and I were elated.

At the end of the night Luis, tears in his eyes, said that he wouldn't accept any pay for the day. I almost forgave him... almost.

Fourteen months later as a Friday night was winding down. I was working the grill and Luis (yes, he was still working for us, and no, I still hadn't forgiven him) was working the ranges. There were about 80 dinners done and "on the spindle" with about 20 more to come in when Eileen, who was hostessing that evening, entered the kitchen and said: "Honey, look what Mrs. O found in her oysters Rockefeller."

Uh oh, announcements like that were usually followed by the presentation of something that didn't belong on or in food: pieces of a scouring pad, bugs, sand, soil, a two inch metal bolt (really), and, worst of all, hair. The discovery of any of these items in a customer's dish would result in profuse apologies, a free meal, and groveling, if requested. Reluctantly, I leaned forward over the line table to look at the object. Oh my God, it was a pearl! Mrs. O had found a pearl in her oysters Rockefeller. It was about the size of a pea and almost perfectly round. The coloring was the expected pearl white but with swirls of light gray, eerily reminiscent of the air in the kitchen 14 months earlier after the Ansel system had released.

At this point a few words about Mrs. O would be in order. Jean Ozyjowski was the science teacher at my kids' elementary school. She had taught my older daughter Alicia, was now teaching my younger daughter Daisy, and would eventually teach my two sons. She was fortyish, with sharp features and a no nonsense manner. Mrs. "O" was respected by her students, and in Daisy's case loved. Led by Daisy, her homeroom class had gotten together money for a birthday present: a gift certificate for dinner for two at the Pump House. She and her husband (a gym teacher at the same school, who had married her after a six year whirlwind courtship) were now enjoying that dinner.

After Eileen left the kitchen I went back to cooking, but couldn't concentrate. Throwing down my spatula and declaring to myself "This is news!" I rushed to my office and searched the yellow pages for the number of the nearest office of the "Star Ledger", New Jerseys' largest newspaper. A reporter listened to my account and agreed that it would make a great story. He had grown up in South Carolina so was no stranger to oyster consumption, yet couldn't recall having heard of any one finding a pearl in one. I then dropped my biggest bomb. "Guess what my daughter has been studying in Mrs. Os' class this past week." "Mollusks?" he tried with a laugh?

 "Yep" I replied.

The story ran in the newspapers Sunday edition, page three, top, under a half page headline. It was picked up by the wire services, and appeared in God knows how many papers across the country (customers and friends told us of phone calls from their acquaintances and relatives all over the country who had read the account in their local paper). The story made both the 6 p.m. and 11 p.m.

news broadcasts on CBS' and ABC's flagship television stations out of New York City. It was read on the Paul Harvey show and many other radio programs.

We had received our fifteen minutes of fame – and then some.

The two incidents that I've just described may seem out of the ordinary to you, but I assure you that, in my business, they are not (Well ok, maybe a little out of the ordinary). They represent the best that the restaurant business has to offer an entrepreneur like me, someone I call a Fezziwig capitalist: The chance to overcome adversity, the rewards (often whimsical) that are earned through hard work, and the character building opportunity to soldier on. This profession, however, can also be cruel to my type of entrepreneur, and had I known that I was a Fezziwig BEFORE I opened my own place things might have turned out very differently.

What is a Fezziwig capitalist? Read on!

CHAPTER 2: WHAT KIND OF CAPITALIST ARE YOU?

What I'm about to present to you is a theory of capitalism that I wish I possessed forty years ago, before I opened my own place. The insights and knowledge that went into this theory came to me in bits and pieces over 49 years in business, 37 of those years spent self- employed.

The framework, the actual building of the theory, was forced on me by a snap decision I made in the spring of 2009. A regular customer of mine named Craig, who with his family owned and operated an advertising agency, stopped by the restaurant with a question. He had a friend who was a professor in Fairleigh Dickinson University's MBA program, from which Craig graduated in 1976. The professor, Dr. Richard Archambault, was teaching a course on entrepreneurship and looking for guest speakers to share their experiences with the class. He had invited a CFO, then a CEO to speak, but had been disappointed with their talks. Craig wasn't surprised by this, and asked the professor why he didn't bring in small-business owners who were actual entrepreneurs, the CFO and CEO being management. "So you're interested then?" replied Dr. Archambault.

Craig's talk was well received, and he asked the professor if he would be amenable to presentations from other small-business owners, specifically Craig's friend who was a concert promoter and ... me.

"Well, are you interested?" asked Craig.

"Sure," I answered. This is my default reply whenever I am asked to do something that sounds interesting, and it's gotten me into trouble on several occasions.

I attended one of Craig's presentations not long afterward and was very impressed. There was lots of razzle-dazzle, including a television ad for his company that starred Terry Bradshaw and a kick-ass PowerPoint presentation. The content was good: he talked about due diligence when purchasing a business and the importance of energy and enthusiasm in success. His list of credentials was impressive: an MBA in accounting, two other successful businesses before his current one, and several awards. I was in big trouble.

The only way I was going to compete with Craig's presentation was to offer something that was different and original. Over the next six months, I began to pull together my theory of the different types of capitalist personalities, drawing on all those bits and pieces. The following is the result.

There seems to be an inclination, lately, among many of those who write about entrepreneurs to define that term very narrowly. These writers feel that only those who create something completely new, a good or service that's never existed before, deserve to be called entrepreneur. I disagree, and so does Webster.

According to Webster's Dictionary an entrepreneur is, "A person who organizes, operates and assumes the risk for business enterprises." My definition (provided in the next paragraph) is similar. That said, I have always been unhappy with the way entrepreneurs (I call them capitalists) were often lumped together in one group, as if Elon Musk were Warren Buffet were me!

There are, I believe, three types of capitalists, and, before continuing, I should give my definition of a capitalist. A capitalist, in this theory, is anyone who starts a business either by purchasing an existing one or creating one, and then runs that business for at least a short time. The start-up of a business I refer to as the entrepreneurial phase, and the running of that business as the managerial phase. I include in the entrepreneurial phase the "shake-out" time, with the managerial phase starting after about a year.

Now you have people in corporate suites and on Wall Street who think that they're capitalists, with their golden parachutes and government bailouts. They're not. For one thing they've never been in the entrepreneurial phase. In addition, if a small businessman/entrepreneur fails he doesn't get severance, he doesn't get a bailout; what he does get is a slap upside the head from Adam Smith's invisible hand. We're the capitalists. There are no safety nets for us. The capitalist, the entrepreneur, the small businessman is the embodiment of the free enterprise system!

At this point, I want to mention one big caveat, and I'll repeat this point later in the book. The three categories that I'll be describing depict pure types. In the real world, there are no pure types. All capitalists are mixes of, at least two, and usually all three of the types.

It's important for an aspiring capitalist to have at least a rough idea of what her mix is, and it's crucial that she know what the predominant type in that mix is. Knowing the mix will save her time, keep her from pursuing dead ends, and eliminate false starts. For this mix will (or should) be one of the most important determinants of what sort of business she'll buy. It will influence where she goes to get financing, and whether or not she takes a partner, and it <u>will</u> determine the way in which she runs her operation. In short, recognizing her own capitalist mix will be the most important step she takes in starting her own business.

Fortunately, for the purposes of this discussion, all three types of capitalists can be found in a work of popular fiction, "A Christmas Carol" by Charles Dickens. That is, two of the types are in the original short story with the third being the creation of Noel Langley. He wrote the screenplay for arguably the most popular film adaptation of the tale, the 1951 "A Christmas Carol" starring Alistair Sim. The characters that represent the three types are Scrooge and Fezziwig from the short story and Mr. Jorkin from the film. I assume that nearly every reader will be familiar with the first two but for those readers that haven't seen that particular screen version, I will take extra care to explain Jorkin's role in the story.

I'd like to start with Fezziwig, however, because I believe that most capitalists are mostly Fezziwigs.

Fezziwig, if you recall, was the owner of a small garment business in 1830s London. He apprenticed the young Scrooge and would keep him in his employ for several years. He is portrayed by Dickens as a kindly, wise and caring boss, liked and respected by all of his employees, including Scrooge. Let us take a look now at those qualities possessed by old Fezziwig that qualify him to be a type. We'll start with motivation using a Q&A format.

Q: What motivates a Fezziwig-type capitalist to go in business for himself?

A: He wants to be his own boss, to meet a payroll instead of a paycheck, to give orders instead of taking them, to do things the right way, HIS WAY. He doesn't enjoy working for others and will usually find a way to own his own shop or rise to the top of a business organization.

Q: What is a Fezziwig's business profile?

A: Fezziwigs are usually passionate about what they do and tend to start businesses that involve an activity that they like or love. A Fezziwig would start small and probably remain that way in order to exert the greatest control over his business. Fezziwigs are normally in the entrepreneurial phase only once or perhaps twice in their business careers, spending the vast majority of those careers in the business management phase. The only way you would find a Fezziwig in the entrepreneurial mode more than once or twice would be if he failed and had to reboot.

Q: Would he take in a partner(s)?

A: He would do well with silent or limited partners, but probably butt heads with an active or general partner. A Fezziwig can get around this problem by splitting up his operation between himself and a partner. This way, the Fezziwig still has the final say in his part of the operation. God help that partner, however, if his part of the operation fails to produce a product that meets the Fezziwig's standards.

Q: How would he manage his business?

A: Like his character in "A Christmas Carol," a Fezziwig might be a fair, compassionate, paternal boss. The kind of boss that would inquire as to your kids' grades in school, invite your family into his home for Christmas, or throw all the employees a holiday party. He could, however, just as easily be an autocratic, selfish tyrant. Doing things the "right way" for his business might not be the right way for his employees. He would tend to be a bad delegator, wanting to keep his hands in everything to make certain that they are done that right way … his way.

If you have experienced "top down" management at your place of employment, your boss is probably a Fezziwig. Top-down, "my way or the highway" management can work well for a small operation, where it's possible for one person to know enough about the business to make all the important decisions. The strong focus and lack of indecision make for competitive advantages. It would probably be inefficient, however, for a large corporation and disastrous for one with horizontal diversification. The best bet for a Fezziwig is to go out on his own, and keep it small and manageable.

Q: How about financing?

A: Fezziwigs tend to look to people they know and trust for money: a relative, friend, or a local banker that he knows from the Rotary Club. A Fezziwig will see the sale of stock or an excessive amount of leverage as diluting his control and be wary of both; this is another reason that they tend to remain small.

*A Fezziwig will seek financing to bet on himself operating in a field in which he has expertise.

Q: What sort of product is he likely to produce?

A: A Fezziwig will take pride in what he does. Reputation means a lot to him, both his reputation with his customers and his peers. A strong Fezziwig (I'll discuss what I mean by strong in chapter six) will even put a reputation for providing a quality product or service above the profit margin. Remember, these guys will spend most of their careers in the management phase, necessitating repeat customers. A reputation for delivering a quality product, and/or providing fine service will count as much as price in bringing people back. Were you to receive bad service or a poor product from a Fezziwig and complained about it, chances are he would do his best to make good.

Q: What are examples of the Fezziwig capitalist?

A: The butcher, the baker, the candlestick maker. Most of the small businesses that you patronize in your hometown, including the professionals (doctors, dentists, and lawyers) are probably owned and operated by a (<u>mostly</u>) Fezziwig. These Fezziwig-owned businesses make the world go 'round, make life palatable. That coffee and bagel that you purchased this morning at 7:10 in your favorite deli, was probably served to you, with a smile and a thank you, by a Fezziwig. (By the way, is it just me, or does "thank you," an expression of appreciation, seem to be disappearing from American retail, replaced by the command "Have a nice day!") You were that Fezziwig's forty-sixth customer, and his day was just getting started. That day began at 4:30 A.M., when he arrived at his business to prep and cook, and he'll probably be there to close up. Without the Fezziwig-type capitalist, the world would come to a sudden, unpleasant stop.

Next let's look at a capitalist who is, in many ways, his foil.

CHAPTER 4 : SCROOGES

Scrooge was portrayed by Dickens as a mean, miserly, odious old sinner, who hated life, hated people and, most of all, hated Christmas. But Scrooge, in my opinion, was given a bum rap. "A Christmas Carol" was written by Dickens in London in 1834. In that place and time, capitalism, while not in its infancy, was at best in early adolescence. The city was often dark at noon from the pollution, Seven-day, twelve-hour-a-day workweeks were the norm. The use of child labor was common, and by child labor we are talking five- and six-year-olds. Dickens saw these shortcomings of capitalism and wrote about them, not in just "A Christmas Carol," but in many of his stories. In those works, he usually assigned the blame for capitalism's shortcomings on the Scrooge-type of capitalist. I think he was mistaken in this,

and my capitalist profile of a Scrooge
will show why.

Q: What motivates a Scrooge-type
capitalist to go in business for himself?

A: Money, Moolah, Bucks, Cabbage!
Now having said this, I'm immediately
going to amend it. Money, you see, is not
really the motivation, it's the measure.
Ted Turner (definitely a strong Scrooge)
said it best in his famous quote, "Life is a
game, and money is how we keep score."
Scrooges are motivated by competition,
they like to win. What they do with their
winnings varies Scrooge by Scrooge, but
they are all driven to win. While many
Scrooges, after achieving success, still
have the first nickel they ever made,
others have given away large portions of
their wealth. Most of the robber barons of
the late-nineteenth and early twentieth
century's gave away substantial amounts
of their fortunes to endow (and get their
names on) colleges, museums, libraries
and art centers. The aforementioned Ted

Turner, whose resume includes winning three America's Cups, starting CNN, and owning the Atlanta Braves, not long ago, gave $1 billion to the United Nations. Bill Gates, Warren Buffet, and Mark Zuckerberg seem to be competing (heh, heh) to see who can give away the most money. Scrooges may or may not be the miser portrayed in the Dickens short story, but they most decidedly are competitors, and there's really no better way to compete, to make a whole boat-load of money, than being in business for yourself.

Q: What is a Scrooge's business profile?

A: Unlike a Fezziwig, a Scrooge will likely avoid going into a business she loves or enjoys. (This is difficult to do and can be a problem for her.). A Scrooge will want to remain dispassionate about her business, ready at the drop of a hat (or profit margin) to sell that business. Picture a scenario where a Scrooge is happily making a nice profit doing something she enjoys, but then sees an opportunity to make an even greater amount of money in a different field. She hesitates because she likes what she is doing, and someone else, who sees the same opportunity, steps up and makes it happen. What you now have is one very unhappy Scrooge.

A Scrooge will be happy spending most of her career in the business management phase, so long as that business is making a nice profit. If not, she's equally willing to enter the entrepreneurial phase over and over if necessary until she finds one that makes enough money. A Scrooge may start small, but will likely get big in a hurry, because she quickly realizes that economies of scale (bigger works better) can make for very nice profits.

Q: Would he take in a partner(s)?

A: Definitely! Silent is fine, if there is no emotional connection; active is even better, for a Scrooge will quickly realize that the more responsibility and work that he can shift to a partner the faster that he can grow.

Q: How would he manage his business?

A: If I had my druthers, I would much prefer working for a Scrooge rather than a Fezziwig. (Take that Mr. Dickens!) For while a Scrooge is unlikely to ask about my children or stop by my house on Christmas with a bottle of cheer, he would be much more likely to offer me advancement and additional responsibility if I showed merit. Scrooges are excellent delegators, realizing that one very good way to make more money is to let talented people help you. Unlike a Fezziwig, you usually know where you stand with a Scrooge; help him increase his profits and you're good.

Q: How about financing?

A: Scrooges will be highly unlikely to look for financing from friends or relations or anyone who could exert any emotional control over them. They need to be nimble and cut and run if the situation calls for it. Stocks, bonds, and banks work best with Scrooges.

* A Scrooge will seek financing to bet on himself operating in a field where he considers himself to be an expert and/or to bet on others who he feels have as much expertise or more than he has in that field.

Q: What sort of product is he likely to produce?

A: A Scrooge will be fine providing a superior product if that's what the market demands. But if he can make money producing a piece of junk, that will be okay too. Am I implying that Scrooges don't care about their reputations? No, but reputation and pride in their product take a back seat to profit margins. Were you to receive bad service or an inferior product from a Scrooge and complained about it, you might get an argument instead of a fix, and the argument might very well end in, "I'll see you in court." A Scrooge will probably spend most of his career in the managerial phase however, necessitating at least some commitment to customer satisfaction.

Q: What are examples of the Scrooge capitalist?

A: Bill Gates, Warren Buffet, Mark Zuckerberg, Ted Turner. Scrooges are the ones that everyone loves to hate, to envy. But while you're gazing at his mansion, when you're drooling over his Maserati, or admiring his $200 haircut take a minute to consider his alternative costs. The concept of alternative costs was one of the first things that I learned in economics back in college. It states that the true cost of something is what one has to give up in order to get it. The next time that you envy a Scrooge, consider how many of his kid's Little League games that he's missed, the recitals passed up, the parties that went unattended, and the wife that never sees him. If that doesn't do it for you, go out and compete with him, and see what it costs YOU.

Wouldn't a Fezziwig have to suffer the same alternative costs? No he wouldn't. How do I know? I lived it.

During the years that my kids were growing up (roughly 1985-2005) our restaurant took a back seat to their needs. Did this cause our business to suffer? Without a doubt! While I was attending the recitals, and coaching sports teams (baseball, softball, and basketball) the restaurant went from being the busiest in town to just average. I was still able, however, to continue to satisfy my primary motivation for self- employment, I was still my own boss. My wife and I were able to get things going again after our youngest left for college, and by 2011 we were once again the hottest place in Hackettstown N.J. (We were also one of the few restaurants to survive the devastating 2008 recession). Under the same circumstances a Scrooge type would have a difficult time satisfying his need to compete and win. A family oriented Scrooge faces some tough choices. He could delay marriage and family (I have a friend who started a business made a bundle, sold said business for another bundle, then retired, married, and started a family). He could involve his family in his business (another acquaintance of mine owns a very successful advertising agency which is co-owned and operated by his wife, his daughter, and his son). But most strong Scrooges must, I believe, content themselves with the knowledge that their wealth has eased their families' journey through life (beautiful home, exotic vacations, the best schools etc.).

 Fezziwigs get a pass in this particular instance but they suffer their own set of alternative costs. The desire to do things the right way, their way, open Fezziwigs to hubris and mediocrity. Their alternative costs come from the advice and help not taken, those costs are the reason that our business stayed small and we never became rich. There are always alternative costs. No one gets to have it all.

Next we'll consider the third type of capitalist. One who, like Scrooge, often gets a bad rap, but who I consider to be the most interesting type of all!

In the 1951 movie "A Christmas Carol," Mr. Jorkin is the CEO (or the 1830s equivalent) of a large London textile company. He tries to buy Mr. Fezziwig's company for what, even Fezziwig must admit, is a very generous offer. Fezziwig declines, however, with "There's more to life than money Mr. Jorkin." Astonished, Jorkin must satisfy himself with pirating Fezziwig's best employee, Scrooge.

Later in the film, Jorkin is accused by his board of directors of embezzlement and is threatened with prison. Scrooge and his co-worker and friend Marley save Jorkin from a trip to "Botany Bay" (an Australian penal colony) with an offer to make good on the amount of money expropriated by Jorkin, in exchange for the right to buy 51% of the company's stock. This shrewd maneuver starts Scrooge on his road to riches. Jorkin, for his part, is relieved but bemused. "It could have been anyone of us. We're all a bunch of thieves under our fancy linen." This is a sentiment shared by at least one present-day Jorkin that I know of.

Q: What motivates a Jorkin-type capitalist to go in business for himself?

A: Risk! A Jorkin is a player, he likes the action, he not only has a tolerance for risk, he craves it! He desires it above money, above control, above just about anything. Being in business for himself can fill that desire quite nicely. You enjoy risk? Boy, have we (entrepreneurs) got risk!

Q: What is a Jorkin's business profile?

A: A Jorkin-type capitalist can get his risk fix in one of two ways. He can start a business that is inherently risky: mercenary troop supplier, an oil-rig wildcatter, a hedge fund, a sunken-treasure recovery company, or anything illegal, in which case he'll spend most of his career in the management phase. This will tend to occur when the second biggest component of his capitalist mix is Fezziwig. He can also get his risk from being in that riskiest of all places, the entrepreneurial phase … as often as possible. This will be the case when he has a sizable amount of Scrooge in his mix. If he remains in the business-management phase, he's likely to remain small. If he chooses to reside in the entrepreneurial phase, he can get very big, very fast.

Q: Would he take in a partner(s)?

A: He would and he should. He's going to need someone to ground him, to reign in his risk taking and monetize his innovations. Scrooges are best.

Q: How would he manage his business?

A: Jorkins are born leaders, charismatic, and inspirational. They are able to get their employees to do things that they wouldn't believe they were capable of, or dare to do. They inspire loyalty and devotion in their employees. Jorkins are usually "big picture" people, not detail oriented, and therefore good delegators.

Q. How will he finance?

A. He'll look for financing anywhere, and the more leverage the better. Hell, he would even go to the mob.

*A Jorkin will seek financing to bet on anything that he has a good feeling about.

Q: What sort of product is he likely to produce?

A: If he gets his risk from remaining in the managerial phase of a risky business, and that business is legal, you can expect the same attitude regarding reputation and providing a quality product that you find with a Fezziwig. You have to remember, however, that bending or breaking the rules is risky and therefore attractive to a Jorkin. Caveat emptor is probably the order of the day for his customers. If he gets his risk by remaining in the entrepreneurial phase, anything goes.

Q: What are examples of the Jorkin capitalist?

A: While I was putting this theory together in 2008, I had been searching for good example of a Jorkin. Then late one evening, as I was watching a CNBC special on the developing financial crisis, there on my television (in handcuffs) was an example of an almost pure Jorkin. When presenting this to those M.B.A. classes, I would ask them to guess who that example was. The hands would shoot up, and they were never wrong. It was Bernie Madoff!

This paints a very negative picture of the Jorkin type, but they are also the big movers and shakers in this world, the innovators. They are the ones willing to take great risk! They're also scarce. Fezziwigs abound, Scrooges while fewer are still numerous, strong Jorkins, though, are a much rarer breed. Instead of Bernie Madoff, think Christopher Columbus, Ferdinand Magellan, Richard Branson, and Elon Musk. But getting back to Mr. Madoff, He is what makes the Jorkin capitalist so interesting. For as reprehensible as Mr. Madoff's actions were, as bad of an actor as he was, if you don't have at least a little bit of old Bernie (or any Jorkin) inside, you don't belong in business for yourself!

That is a pretty darn good segue into the chapter on risk.

But before we go there, I would like to make this personal.

CHAPTER 6: CONFESSIONS OF A CLOSET FEZZIWIG

You've seen (and will see) me refer to people as strong Scrooges or strong Fezziwigs or Jorkins. How do I arrive at these characterizations? Simply put, they're guesses. The only mix that I'm certain of is mine. Speculating on another's mix is fun and can be of some value at times. For instance, when making an important purchase of a good or service, it can help in negotiations to have an idea of the counter-party's capitalist mix. But it's just a guess. You are, however, certainly capable of ascertaining your own mix.

To find that mix, you're going to have to be honest with yourself (an adult beverage or two might help here). What's your motivation? Are you contemplating going into business for yourself because you just don't like working for someone? Is it because you'd rather be working to make yourself rich instead of your boss? Is it because the idea of owning your own business is just sooo exciting? Or is it all or most of the above? If it's the last, and it almost certainly is, which motivation is the strongest?

Beyond motivation, consider the other questions (excluding "examples") that I've asked of each type. Which answers most closely mirror what your response would be? If you find yourself in general agreement with three of the five answers to one type's questions, then that's the predominant type in your mix. If you (mostly) agree with four of the five or five out of five, then you're a strong version of that type. If you don't **fully** agree with all five of one type's answers, you are, like everyone else, a mix. You must then look to the answers provided by the other two capitalist types to round out that mix.

Don't expect to nail your mix exactly. It's **very** important, however, that you determine the predominate type in that mix. The most important answer in divining your predominate type is the one to the question on motivation. If you find that you don't fully agree with a given answer but lean in its direction, that's okay. There are no pure types, remember? And this is not an exact science. It's impossible to completely quantify human behavior, although, Lord knows, we do try. Go with your gut.

Having difficulty deciding on which is your predominate type? Do you find that you agree with a couple of questions from each of the three types? Congratulations, you might just be a "super-capitalist"!

Picture this; a risk taking innovator (Jorkin) who can effectively monetize his innovations (Scrooge), then consistently deliver them as beautiful products at a reasonable price (Fezziwig). I knew such a person. He seemed to move effortlessly from one venture to another, making lots of money on almost all of them. We ALL know another example....Steve Jobs

Jobs wasn't perfect, some of his innovations weren't well received, he could be stubborn about sticking to price points that didn't make sense, and a few of his products developed serious glitches. But when he was on his game boy oh boy was he one awesome capitalist! My guess as to his capitalist mix? 40% Jorkin, 30% Scrooge, 30% Fezziwig. Despite this rather even distribution of the three types in his capital mix Jobs was first and foremost a Jorkin and he was smart enough to realize it. He chose to go into a field that rewarded innovation and risk taking, then he used the strengths from the other two parts of his capitalist mix to turn that industry on its' head.

In Chapters Eight and Nine, I'll cover what business opportunities and situations that you should embrace or avoid both during the start-up, and the running of your business, depending on your capitalist mix.

But now it's time to get to the personal part. I am, as I mentioned earlier, a Fezziwig, or more accurately, mostly a Fezziwig. I'd say that I was 60% Fezziwig, 25% Scrooge and 15% Jorkin. My motivation is primarily to be my own boss, but I take some pleasure in competing, and have just enough of a taste for risk and uncertainty to have lasted 37 years in business for myself. I mostly agree with four of the five Fezziwig answers and partly agree with the fifth. (I based those questions and answers not only on my own experience but on that of other capitalists whose motivations were both similar and different from mine).

Had I realized and accepted my mix before I started my own business, I almost certainly would have chosen a different one. Prior to opening my business, I had assumed that I was a

Scrooge, although I wouldn't have put it that way back then. I remember bragging to my friends about how I would make my first million (this was a big deal back in the seventies) by thirty-five, and be rich by forty. It wasn't until several years after we opened the restaurant that I began to fully fathom what my capitalist nature was. This happened over time, starting with my years of employment at The Friar Tuck Inn in Cedar Grove, New Jersey.

I had worked at the "Tuck" the last Two years of high school and throughout college, rising from busboy to maitre'd. After a short stint at NYU's graduate school of business (where, like Garp I gradually decided that I no longer wanted to be in school), I accepted an offer from the owner of Friar Tuck, Francis J. Jacobs Jr, to manage the place.

I was definitely what you would call a "hands on manager" It was a big restaurant with six banquet rooms and two public dining areas, and I was everywhere, wanting everything to be perfect. Customer satisfaction was my first priority. I would often over-staff, running up costs, in order to ensure that everything went well.

I particularly enjoyed running the banquet end of Jacob's business as private parties were much easier to manage efficiently compared to the "ala carte" rooms. On a busy Saturday night I would have to co-ordinate the serving of 500 dinners within an hour or two, oversee the actions of the maître ds, waiters, bartenders, and kitchen help, and make certain the three or four bridal parties NEVER came in contact with one another. I loved it. With a banquet you knew what to expect, how many guests you'd be serving and what time they would arrive. All that was required was some thorough advance planning. Ala carte was chaotic, you could do 150 "covers" in a couple of hours or 50 dinners spread out all evening. Staffing and satisfying the customers could be a real challenge.

Jacobs (Jake) was about as supportive and understanding as a boss could be but I still chaffed under his supervision. When after five years I decided to leave and open a place of my own I chose as a partner a friend who had worked with me at "The Tuck" during my college years. Bob was hard working, intelligent, and honest, traits that should have made him an ideal partner. But from the beginning of our relationship I demanded that things be done my way. Things got so bad that at the end a busy Saturday night about three years after we opened our restaurant, Bob asked that we have a little talk. "Rodg" he said "I didn't go into business to work for somebody else!" In an effort to make sure that things went well during that difficult evening I had been demanding that everyone do exactly as I said, including Bob.

It finally began to dawn on me that there were certain things that I required to be happy in my business. I needed to be in charge and customer satisfaction had to be my first priority. The biggest revelation, however, originated from the business that I had chosen before becoming fully aware of my capitalist mix! The restaurant that Bob and I had opened was an ala carte restaurant. We had considered purchasing a banquet facility but lacked the necessary capital (banquet halls require a lot of brick and mortar).

The a la carte business is trendy! More trendy than any other business, with the possible exception of fashion. Trendy and Fezziwigs don't mix. Let me give you an example of a conversation that I think – no, that I'm certain – took place in and around Hackettstown, N.J., every Saturday about 4 p.m.

He: *"Honey where do you want to go for dinner tonight?"*

She: *"Oh! Let's go to the Pump House, the food there is so good, I love that one waitress, Bridget, and they have that table that overlooks the water, remember?"*

He: *"Nah, we go there all the time. Why don't we try that new Bulgarian-Guatemalan fusion place that just opened on Main Street?"*

Now, this is the sort of thing that can bring a Fezziwig to tears, break his heart. Was all his work trying to put out the best product possible for nothing? Don't they realize how hard he's worked (sob!) to make certain that they received good value each and every time that they dined at his place?

But it's logical! In return for a new experience, what does that couple have to lose if their dinner stinks? Forty to fifty bucks, maybe twenty more if the place has a liquor license. Ah, but what if their daughter's wedding reception is a bomb?

Now you're talking $20,000.00, $25,000.00, maybe more. The banquet business is built on reputation, the reputation earned through a quality product consistently delivered. Banquets are right in a Fezziwig's wheelhouse.

So…If I'd known all those years ago that I was a Fezziwig, I could have waited a little longer, accumulated a little more money, and opened a catering facility. Perhaps today, rather than having spent 37 years constantly reinventing my business to fit the latest ala carte trend , I would be the catering king of North Jersey. Perhaps not, after all I am a strong Fezziwig and probably would have kept it to one place and kept that place small and controllable. But I almost certainly would have enjoyed my business more!

Don't get me wrong, the ala carte restaurant business has provided my wife and I with a ton of excitement (see the first chapter) and a strong sense of accomplishment. Since we sold our restaurant, it's rare that more than a few days pass without encountering former customers who tell us how much they enjoyed eating at our place, and how much they miss us. The Pump House also provided my family with a good and relatively stable income for 37 years. I'm fairly certain, however, that we could have achieved the same, or better results in a field that was a little less exciting and a lot more predictable, and where success was a lot more dependent on doing things the right way....my way.

There are ways of picking a business to go into that will compliment your personal capitalist mix (to be discussed in chapter 9). Discover that mix before you make your move!

At this juncture, you might be asking "Once he realized what his mix was, why didn't he sell his place and buy a banquet hall?" The answer is that by the time I realized my capitalist personality my risk tolerance had fallen below the level required to start anew. Why?

Another great segue! This time let's take it and consider risk.

CHAPTER 7: RISK

Risk is defined by Wikipedia as "A consequence of action taken in spite of uncertainty…The exposure to the possibility of loss, injury, or other adverse or unwelcome circumstance." Risk tolerance is defined as how much risk one is willing and able to stand.

Man has been attempting to quantify both risk and risk tolerance for at least the past 100 years with limited success. The measurement of risk tolerance, the Holy Grail of the financial services industry, has proved to be particularly elusive. The various models designed to predict their clients risk tolerance have, for the most part, yielded a level of satisfaction no greater than the level achieved without the use of said models.

Some insights have been gained, however. It's been discovered, for instance, that risk behavior doesn't necessarily transfer from one genre to another. That is, if you seek risk in physical activities, say sky diving, that attitude may or may not transfer to financial risk taking. If you like to gamble at the casino you might not enjoy gambling on a new business. It has also been shown that long term exposure to uncertainty can make an individual less risk tolerant. Age, personal finances, marital status, number of dependents, and gender also affect risk tolerance. The younger you are, the more risk tolerant. The greater your financial cushion the riskier you will be. Singles can absorb more risk. The fewer the number of dependents the greater the risk tolerance, and, yes, guys, you take more risk - slightly more.

From my personal experience and my talks with other capitalists I have arrived at my own set of risk tolerance conclusions. They are anecdotal and not scientifically rigorous but I believe that they are valid, and will be of use to you.

1. You will experience a type of risk in the entrepreneurial phase that's different from that in the managerial phase.

2. The risk in the entrepreneurial phase is more intense and shorter than in the managerial phase. This risk is based more on possible loss than uncertainty.

3. The risk in the managerial phase will be based more on uncertainty, less intense, and, depending on your capitalist mix, last **much** longer.

4. Regardless of your capitalist mix, or level of risk tolerance, entrepreneurial-risk is easier to deal with than managerial risk.

5. The type of risk that will predominate in your career, and to a somewhat lesser degree your tolerance to that risk will be determined by you capitalist mix.

6. Entrepreneurial risk is tough, managerial is tougher.

Let's consider the risk encountered in the entrepreneurial phase first. The level of risk here will be high. The commerce department estimates that 60% of all new businesses will fail in the first year. The intensity of that risk will depend on the amount of money involved, the time invested, your various personal responsibilities and the level of commitment. More money invested equals more risk. Full-time commitment involves more risk than if you keep your day job. More risk will be borne by a single entrepreneur than by a group of investors, the greater your personal responsibilities the lower your risk tolerance. The level of this risk will also be determined by your capitalist mix. Fezziwigs will normally only be in this phase once or twice but will also tend to go it alone shouldering most of the risk themselves. Scrooges on the other hand will spend much more time in the entrepreneurial phase yet will be more likely to take on partners thereby spreading the risk. Jorkins? Well a Jorkin, depending on the amount of that type in his mix, will find himself somewhere between indifference to the risk and seeking more of it. .

Managerial risk is very different.

Picture it this way, entrepreneurial risk can be compared to a roller-coaster ride, managerial to a long commute in heavy traffic during an ice storm. The former can be terrifying the latter will wear you down. It's the one that wears you down that I'll be focusing most of my attention on the rest of this chapter, and here's why.

Worry! Worry is the symptom of managerial risk, and unless you can handle worry, and its effects on your performance and your well- being, you don't belong in business for yourself!

You **will** worry. You'll worry about the economy, the competition that just opened across the street, your unpaid bills, and government regulations. Even the weather, when snow was predicted for Saturday night I needed to be sedated. There's no shortage of things to worry about **and** we're the ones with no safety net, remember? How you deal with this worry, both its physical effects on you, and the way that it impacts your performance is the most important part of your risk tolerance.

7. This is a good time to draw a distinction between risk tolerance and courage, and I'm talking to you macho men out there! Courage is:

* The ability to "keep your head when all those around you are losing theirs, and blaming it on you." (Kipling's "If")

* Sticking to your principals when doing so will cost you dearly.

* Keeping your humanity when what you're facing demands that you abandon it.

Entrepreneurial and managerial risk tolerance are measures of how well you handle worry and possible financial loss, no more, no less.

Courage is special, something to yearn for. The ability to adapt to loss and worry, to take it in stride, is a nice trait to possess, sort of like the ability to recognize a bargain when you see one. Yet it's really not that important, unless… you want to start a business. Then you must be honest with yourself in rating your ability to handle worry, because it **will** be a factor in determining how successful your business is, and how happy that you are in what you do.

Ok, so aspiring entrepreneurs (even Jorkins) need to be aware of their level of managerial risk tolerance before going into business for themselves. How do they know if they have enough?

I have a test.

In order to take the test I'm going to ask you to recall events in which you experienced anxiety over your eventual performance (athletic events, recitals, important tests, speeches)

IF YOUR EVENTUAL PERFORMANCE WAS GOOD:

Did your level of anxiety decrease, and eventually disappear as the event drew nearer? If yes, give yourself 5 points

Did your level of anxiety decrease but never quite disappear? 4 points

Did it remain the same throughout? 3 points

Did it increase as the event neared? 2 points

IF YOUR EVENTUAL PERFORMANCE WAS ADEQUATE

Did your anxiety level decrease and go away? 4 points

Did it decrease but remain? 3 points

Did it stay steady? 2 points

Did it keep increasing? 1 point

IF YOUR PERFORMANCE WAS POOR

Disappear? 2 points

Just decrease? 1 point

Remain steady? 0

Increase? -2 points

Analyze as many challenging events as you can, and add up your score and divide by the number of events.

If your average is 3.0 or greater in my opinion your risk tolerance is sufficient to handle self-employment.

AMPLFICATIONS, EXPLANATIONS, AND CAVEATS

1. The more events that you can score, the more valid the results.

2. Should your results, in either performance or anxiety level, show improvement over time (the event scored from last year was better than the one from the year before, which was better than the previous one) you can ignore the score, you're good to go. Adaptability to worry trumps all!

3 . Don't be afraid to give yourself half points. If, for example, your anxiety decreases but doesn't go away and your performance was **very** good give yourself a 4.5 rather than a 4. Again, quantifying human behavior is inexact, an art.

4. As was the case in my capitalist types Q&A I make no scientific claims for this test. It's based on my personal experience and input from other small business owners.

5. If you have a significant other, have them take the test. You may be happy as a clam taking on managerial risk, but your partner may be staying awake at night worrying for you.

6. Your tolerance of managerial risk will affect not only your performance and well-being but your willingness to take on entrepreneurial risk as well. If you have trouble handling managerial risk it can have a corrosive effect on your ability to take on new entrepreneurial risk.

7 .If you're a neat freak beware, neither the entrepreneurial nor managerial phases are ever neat and orderly. There is a loose correlation between neatness and risk aversion.

8 .If you didn't score well on the test don't despair, think of a low score as a heads up rather than a disqualifier. While there are people who can take all the worry in stride (unpaid bills, competition, new government regulations, SNOW!) and I know some who can, these lucky

individuals are few and far between. The rest of us deal with uncertainty with fallbacks such as;

"Not to worry, I'm sure that I'll come up with something" (me)

"Well it seemed pretty bad yesterday but today I feel better about it" (my wife)

"I won't worry about it today, I'll worry tomorrow" (Scarlet O'Hara)

So if you scored poorly on the test there's a good chance that you'll adapt.

But YOU WILL experience the worry, and unlike entrepreneurial risk you won't be able to share it with, or dish it off to anyone else.

Frank Hyneman Knight in his ground-breaking book on economics "Uncertainty and Profit" put his finger on the relationship between risk assumption and the entrepreneur when he states "Profit earned by the entrepreneur who makes decisions in an uncertain environment is the entrepreneurs reward for bearing uninsurable risk"." Uninsurable risk" being his way of saying no safety net. The entrepreneur is the one who deals with the risk, an employee, no matter how important or "key" risks only his job; the owner puts much more on the line. Risk and ones tolerance for it are at the very heart of the entrepreneurial experience.

The entrepreneur is becoming something of an endangered species. According to a September '14 Los Angeles Times article by Walter Hamilton "The image of the U.S. as bursting with entrepreneurial zeal, is more myth than reality. In truth, the rate at which new companies are being formed has fallen steadily during the past three decades."...."It's down everywhere. In every locale, in every industry"..."as a share of all businesses or relative to the size of the working age population –it has fallen in half."

The article lists several reasons for this, the first being an increase in risk aversion. If that's true I'll bet that much of the risk aversion is misplaced. According to the article people are put off by entrepreneurial risk, the sheer terror of the start-up, and while I don't mean to trivialize this risk, it can be dealt with by most. It's short lived, therefore so are it's ill effects. As I related earlier, the effects that this risk may have on your performance can be ameliorated by delegating (even for Fezziwigs). There are many professionals involved in the start-up, lawyers, Realtors, contractors, local officials, and bankers. Many of these professionals will be more than happy to participate in decision making, indeed some will demand a say (town officials and bankers). The deleterious effects on your health and well- being will also be minimized by the relatively short duration of entrepreneurial risk. You can simply "brass it out". It's the risk that aspiring owners are unaware of that can make or break their business, managerial risk.

In my case, when I started my business I was;

*30 years old.

*Single.

*Renting an apartment.

*Aided in my start-up by a partner, a good accountant, and a very good lawyer.

By the time that I'd realized what my capitalist mix I was;

*Over 40.

*Married with four children.

*Without a partner.

*Most importantly, suffering from over ten years of managerial risk.

I just didn't have enough risk tolerance to pull the trigger on a new start-up.

If only I had realized what my capitalist mix was at the beginning of my self-employment!

In a highly sited paper on entrepreneurship and risk tolerance by economists H.K.Hvide and Georgies Panos it was found that while risk seeking individuals formed more new companies than risk adverse people, they also tended to do worse once the business was up and running. In an attempt to explain this they offered that perhaps the risk seekers were over-confident or were willing to accept a lower level of compensation for the risk taken. I have another explanation: Entrepreneurial risk isn't the same as managerial, and tolerance for one doesn't imply tolerance for the other.

On a more optimistic note several studies on managerial risk (they don't call it this), including a huge study (200,000 participants over 22 years) by another Teutonic economist. W. Hyll, have indicated that risk adverse people can adapt to worry over time! My personal experience confirms this. My managerial risk tolerance did improve over time, but that risk affected my entrepreneurial risk tolerance.

I realize that these observations skew towards the Fezziwig type of capitalist, as he is likely to spend almost all of his career in the managerial phase. Scrooges, however don't get a pass here, for while a Scrooge will probably spend a lot more time in the entrepreneurial phase than a Fezziwig will, he will still be in the managerial phase for most of his career. Jorkins with a lot of Fezziwig in their mix will also need to deal with managerial risk.

Finally, **if** you have the requisite amount of managerial risk tolerance, and **if** you're aware of your capitalist mix, your odds of success will be high, as will the level of satisfaction derived from your endeavors.

You'll be "Self-employed and Loving it!

Now let's get a little more specific about what's right for your particular capitalist mix.

CHAPTER 8: SUMMING UP, WHAT'S RIGHT FOR YOU

In this chapter I will describe some "big picture" parameters for each capitalist type and then in the following chapter, I'll focus on more specific advice.

I'd like to begin, once more, with the Fezziewig type capitalist, but before I do I'd like to take you back to that caveat I provided at the beginning of the book, namely "THERE ARE NO PURE TYPES". You will need to approach these parameters in the context of your capitalist mix (I know you've figured that out by now). For example, if you see yourself as a strong Fezziwig you should embrace the Fezziwig parameters as they'll most certainly apply. If however you see yourself as more of a mix, with Fezziwig barely edging out one of the others -let's say Fezziwig 45%, Scrooge 40% and Jorkin 15%- then you should give the Fezziwig parameters their due attention but try to blend them with the Scrooge parameters that fit. Jorkin at 15% you can skim through.

So......if you're a Fezziwig;

* Find your niche.

Look to start your business in an area that is relatively stable and hard to disrupt Pick a field where craftsmanship and expertise are rewarded, where economies of scale (bigger) are not only unimportant but an actual disadvantage. When creating a business or considering the purchase of an existing one, ask yourself: can I put my personal stamp on this business? Can I efficiently manage this business?

* Micro- innovate often.

You can (and should) innovate in your business. Accept that your innovation will probably occur within the general parameters of your industry, but don't fall into the trap of "This is the way we've always done it," a big temptation for Fezziwigs.

* You'll do better with fewer employees.

Despite their pluses (bringing new perspective and energy to your business, freeing you up to do more important things, or to take some time off) an employee will never do a job as well as you would. They don't have the incentive; it's not their place. This will drive you nuts.

* Expect to have only one place of business.

More than one will stretch you too thin, leading to a decrease in the quality of your product. This will also drive you nuts.

* Follow your passion

This works for a Fezziwig. There are pitfalls, however, even for him (I go into more detail on this in the next chapter). A business involving the arts, a craft, or a trade will likely fall under this parameter. Sports, hobbies, and collecting fit here as well. How about book writing?

* Customer satisfaction will most likely be your primary motivator.

Just as money is the measure of competitive success for a Scrooge, customer satisfaction will be a barometer for a Fezziwig of how "doing it the right" way is working out.

In their book THEY MADE AMERICA which chronicles the inventors and innovators (mostly Jorkins) who made America an economic powerhouse, the author Harold Evans channels Adam Smith, the high priest of capitalism and the industrial revolution, to provide a description of this Fezziwig parameter. "He (Smith) noted that as soon as a producer of goods – Smith called him an 'artificer' –had acquired more than he needed, he did not extend his own business. He was not tempted by large wages and the easy subsistence that this might bring. He feels that the artificer is the servant of his customer from whom he derives his subsistence."

* Beware of active (general) partners.

They will have the incentive of ownership but it's inevitable that that there will be disagreements with you on the right way to do things, and this will be a big problem for you.

* Look for funding from people or firms that have an interest only in return.

They can't have any interest in running things or even offering input. Believe it or not, if you're a strong Fezziwig, you'd probably rather face foreclosure than allow someone to tell you how to fix things.

* Because of all the above, resign yourself to making a good living rather than becoming rich.

A decent living, along with building a reputation for providing a fine product, will be enough, trust me.

Now let's consider the Scrooge Capitalist;

* Grow baby grow

Outside of a monopoly (illegal unless government sanctioned), growth is the surest path to wealth. Some industries are better suited to growth than others. A good or service that lends itself to regimentation, that can be mass produced or franchised is for you. Before starting a business, ask yourself; can it be quickly grown? Can it attract adequate funding?

*Within the limits of running an efficient operation, the more employees the merrier.

A Scrooge will usually look to get larger to increase revenue and profit, and while he's likely be ruthless when it comes to matters of productivity there is just so much that he can get out of an employee. Sooner or later he has to hire. He will embrace innovative and hard working employees offering them advancement right up to a partnership.

 * Growth in revenue (and profit) will be the major driver for you.

This is a Scrooges report card, her ultimate measure of success. "Top" line growth will give her temporary satisfaction but maximizing "bottom line" profit is the quest.

* Be wary of following your passion

I covered this in chapter one. If you're a strong Scrooge, starting a business that involves an activity that you love can limit your opportunities. There are exceptions to this rule, particularly if the Fezziwig component of your capitalist mix is substantial. Two examples that come immediately to mind: Arnold Palmer was a huge success in his many golf related businesses, and Danny Meyer has built a restaurant empire. But in general, keeping yourself open to new start-up options will make meeting your financial goals much easier

* Funding from friends or relatives will make you cautious, slow to react to changes and new opportunities.

This is kryptonite to a Scrooge.

* Be aware going in that your alternative costs regarding raising a family can be high.

As I discussed in the chapter 3, there are ways to ameliorate this: Delay marriage, have fewer kids, bring members of your family into the business. But there will be conflict between maximizing profit and familial obligations. About half of the dramas coming out of Hollywood and on TV use this for a story line. This is something that you need to come to grips with before you start your business, and if you're married, something to be discussed and a path agreed upon with your spouse.

* Look to partner up

Scrooges are much more amenable to general partners than the other two capitalist types. Partnership will bring to your operation someone whose incentive to succeed is equal to yours, in effect doubling your competitiveness. Even strong Scrooges blend well with other Scrooges or the other two types.

* Embrace the beat down

This was a favorite expression of Arnold Swarzenegger and it referred to how he felt you should deal with envy. The greater your success the more of this emotion that you'll face. This can cause a sensitive Scrooge to play down his accomplishments. My view on this matches that of Zero Mostel in "The Producers", "If you got it, flaunt it baby!"

Now for the Jorkins out there...

* New is the new new.

If the second biggest part of your capitalist mix is Scrooge, any scientific break-through should be studied for practical applications. A new product, new service, new way to deliver or disrupt an existing good or service is for you. Bending conventional behavior or wisdom should be your passion. Any industry that is big and set in its' ways should fall in your crosshairs. Before purchasing a business ask yourself :Can this business be fundamentally changed or disrupted.

* Spend your life in the fast lane

If the second largest part of your capitalist mix is Fezziwig, any operation that puts at risk life and limb and/or fortune should be right up your alley. Before starting a business you should ask yourself; do people avoid this field because its's risky?

* **Be prepared to fail.**

If you get your risk fix from spending lots of time in the entrepreneurial phase you're going to fail more (possibly much more) than you succeed. Examples of this are so common among Jorkins that I'm tempted to give examples of those that don't fail often.

A few of those that have failed; Henry Ford, Walt Disney, Milton Hershey, H.J.Hienz

*Because of the above, be prepared for the possibility that you may spend part of your career impoverished.

Take heart however as most Jorkins manage to turn things around. Again there are many examples: Nickola Tesla, George Forman, MC Hammer, Gary Kildal, Charles Goodyear, Dan Bricklin

* **Ignore the naysayers**.

There will many and many of these. Some of them will be legitimately concerned about your welfare; others will be motivated by jealousy of your ability to handle the risk. You will need someone to give you honest feedback on your ventures (see below), but it must be a person that **you** choose.

* Bend the rules, don't break them.

This needs to be addressed by all strong Jorkins as it has led to the demise of many of them.

Those that bent the rules (disrupters); Jeff Bezos, Travis Kalanick, Garret Camp and Steve Jobs.

Those that broke them (felons); Bernie Madoff, Jordan Belford, Kim Dotcom.

*Look to partner with Scrooges.

A strong Scrooge will bring financial focus to your various innovations and schemes. He'll also know when to "hold-em and know when to fold-em", and you'll need someone to keep you under some sort of control. A Fezziwig would also work, but a strong one won't have you.

Okay, enough of the big picture; now it's (finally!) time to get down to some specific advice.

CHAPTER 9: DOS AND DON'TS

In the first part of this chapter the advice that I'll be giving is generic. It will apply to most if not all small businesses, and is equally relevant to all three types of capitalists. Later, my advice will be capitalist type specific. The suggestions are the result of not only my experiences at my restaurant, but my observations of the practices of the many small businesses that I dealt with over 37 years.

These dos and don'ts are listed in no particular order, as I feel that they are more or less of equal value.

*Don't collect on accounts receivable yourself

As the owner of your own business, you will be wearing many hats. One of those hats will belong to the company's leading (only?) salesman. Certainly at the beginning and probably for quite a while you will do all or most of the selling of your firms' product or service. You will be the "face" of your business. **Don't** put a scowl on that face! If you, the company's owner, collect on the due and often over-due bills, you are going to wind up alienating customers. When they see your name on the caller ID they won't pick up. If they see you coming up their front steps they'll disappear. They will come to fear you and resent you, even after they get current with your bills. How in the world will you ever be able to sell to them again?

While we're on the subject, as your business grows and you're able to afford to hire sales-people don't have them act as bill collectors either! Let me give an example of how bill collection should work.

Long ago when I worked at The Friar Tuck Inn I was able to observe accounts receivable management at its best. This occurred in the late 60's when "Jake" the owner had just instituted a house credit card. This, by the way, was a radical and innovative move as credit cards were then just catching on. Jake put one of his secretaries Eileen Kochems in charge of collections from the card holders. I had the opportunity to watch, or rather hear her in action one afternoon when I was in the offices on an errand for him. She was on the phone with a delinquent account, and let me just say that I was *sooo* glad that I wasn't on the other end of that line. Tapping Ms. Kochems (0r the Dragon Lady as some of the employees at the restaurant called her) for this duty was smart move number two for Jake. For if that person on the other end of that call came in the restaurant later that day with the intention of throwing what he owed in the face of the person that dunned him, and then vowing to never set foot in the place again, Jake could have taken that irate individual to the bar, bought him a drink, joked about the often over-zealous Dragon Lady, smoothed him over, collected the money and kept him as a customer. It was an anonymous employee, not Jake who had insulted the guy.

Do not collect on the bills yourself, get someone else to do it, someone nasty. Let your mother-in-law do it.

You are probably saying to yourself at this point "well no duh", but you would be amazed at the number of small businesses that make this mistake.

*Don't use a "telephone" tree in lieu of a real person to answer calls during regular business hours

A "telephone tree" is accepted and appreciated by customers that call after your business has closed for the day, but I don't know of **anyone** who likes having to go through one when you're open. Yet in the past twenty years or so these annoying things have virtually replaced the receptionist. I believe that this is one of those "monkey see, monkey do" deals, going something like this: "R.J., have you heard? Our competition has just replaced their receptionist with an answering machine and they're saving a bundle!" (around $300. a week if **all** that person did was answer the phone.)

" Really B.K.? Well two can play that game, we'll get one too."

No! In my opinion this is just nuts. You should never cut costs in a way that results in lost revenue. Assign an employee to answer the phone or better yet you answer it- don't let your mother-in-law answer it.

*Don't do the books yourself

This is a big temptation that needs to be resisted for the following reasons. As I stated previously, you're going to be wearing many hats the first few years after you open, and the most important role that you'll play is that of salesman. Without revenue you have no business. You must sell, sell, and then sell some more to get your business going. All your time should be taken up with selling. In addition, doing the books can make you cautious and those first years you can't afford (pun intended) to be cautious. Buy that round of drinks for some prospective clients, book that tee time at the expensive golf course, make reservations at the swanky restaurant, run that powerful, but expensive radio ad and sell!

Give the bookkeeping to someone that you trust, someone who's responsible, left-brained, and who knows when to hit the panic button, then forget about it and get out there and sell.

Pay your bills weekly if at all possible

Here we will bow down before the great god Cash Flow. I get a kick out of reading books authored by former CEOs who went into business for themselves and were shocked, yes shocked at how important cash flow was to their businesses. Cash flow, or more accurately the lack thereof, is that important, is only tangentially related to profit, and has been the ruin of many an otherwise healthy concern.

When you first meet the purveyors that you need to supply your business they will probably offer you "net thirty", meaning that you'll have a month after delivery of their product to pay their invoice. Sounds good doesn't it? You get to use their money for thirty days. What's not to like about that?

Plenty! Unless your bookkeeper is tough as nails net thirty is guaranteed to get you into cash flow trouble. Nearly all new businesses (outside of Silicon Valley) have difficulty setting up lines of credit with their bankers, who demand experience before approval. Given that, this is how it works, or, more accurately, doesn't work.

Let's assume that your new business is booming- as it generally will be after the initial kinks are ironed out-and revenue is steadily increasing month after month. This will cause the following to happen; you'll wind up paying the bills that were incurred from generating let's say x amount of revenue in month one with the revenue from month two which is 2x, then paying that months bills with the revenue from month three which turns out to be 4x. Even if your costs are an abysmal 100% of revenue you have lots of cash lying around. Despite your frantic bookkeepers warnings you will spend that money. If you're good you'll spend it on the business, if you're naughty you'll spend it on yourself, but you will spend it.

Then the business levels off and even declines a little. This **will** happen eventually, either for cyclical reasons- a recession or simply a slow time of year (in the restaurant business January and February stink) or for secular reasons; you're no longer the new kid on the block and folks are beginning to tire of your product, or you've got some new, potent competition. Now the following happen: You're now responsible for month tens' bills used to build 18x of revenue and pay them with month elevens' revenue which is 16x. The following month you do 11x. Unless your cost percentage is excellent you will find yourself short of cash with nowhere to turn (except a credit card that charges 29% interest) until business picks back up.

This, as I mentioned before, can cause your business to fail! If you pay your bills weekly things will still get tight when revenue falls, but you'll become aware of the problem earlier and will hopefully be able to deal with it (cut costs, innovate) before the bookkeeper jumps out the window.

*After you've been in business for five years you have three options (I wanted to say three years, but didn't want to appear hysterical)

1. Innovate

2. Sell the business

3 . Remain the same and resign yourself to steadily declining sales.

This is certainly the case in the a la carte restaurant business, and seems to hold sway in many other fields of endeavor. The time that elapses before the revenue declines may vary, but unless you innovate it will happen.

* Never give someone who has been dishonest with you a second chance.

Never! I've made this mistake and so have most of my self-employed acquaintances. Regardless of how sincere and heartfelt the apology ,no matter how much they need the job, if they've lied or stolen once they **will** do it again.

Next I'll be making suggestions that are specific to one or more of the three types of capitalist. After each suggestion I will assign an f for Fezziwig, an s for Scrooge and a j for Jorkin depending on whether it applies to them. To further narrow the applicability, I'll assign either a capital or lower case to those letters, a capital denoting very applicable, lowercase somewhat less so.

*Guard against hidden partners.

If you're planning on delegating a significant amount of authority and responsibility, make certain that you have a controller or bookkeeper that you trust completely to over-see the organizations funds, or you'll wind up with a partner(s) that you don't know about. **S**, f, **J**

*Don't "nickel and dime" the customer.

I'm going to put a lower case s at the end of this, but that s really stands for stubborn rather than Scrooge. When I've run this piece of advice past Scrooges more often than not I've confronted a red face and the admonition that "I'm full of doo doo". But I stand by my belief that this should apply to Scrooges as well as the other two types. If your approach is to welcome a customer in, then try to separate him from as much of his money as you possibly can and send him on his way, you're not going to see him again. This practice is not conducive to repeat business! Scrooges like Fezziwigs and some Jorkins will wind up spending the majority of their careers in the management phase, and in most instances will be in need of repeat business and/or referrals.

In the restaurant business, this practice takes the form of "up-selling".

Customer- " I'd like a vodka and tonic please."

Waiter- "Would you like to make that a Kettle and tonic?"

Customer- "Uh… ok."

The customer here had two choices: He could say no, and appear a cheapskate to the person sitting across from him or the group that he's with, or he could suck it up and spring for the extra two bucks. Either way he's pissed and will remember it. The owner has gained a couple of bucks and probably lost a patron. This practice (and it's very popular) is, in my opinion, the essence of "penny wise and pound foolish". The customer always realizes that he's being taken advantage of, no matter how cleverly the fleecing is disguised. **F.** s. j.

* Try not to start your business on a shoestring.

Under-capitalization is a guarantee of slow growth. Building up your business through working capital is a slow go (take it from me). **S. J.** f.

* Put that capital where it belongs.

Any money that goes towards selling to or impressing the customer is well spent. Money used to impress your friends, your employees or yourself is wasted. **F S** j

*Follow your passion?

This piece of advice is thrown out in books and articles on entrepreneurship, but it's flawed. First of all there is no surer way to lose your passion for something than making it your source of income. If I had a nickel for every home cook who wanted to open their own restaurant I wouldn't need to write this book. The difference between cooking for a dozen of your friends and putting out 125 dinners in three hours on a Saturday night is like night and day. Then there is my earlier admonition to avoid falling in love with what you do, it will destroy your ability to pick up on new opportunities. **S. J.** f.

*Taking on an active partner is not unlike getting married.

*Entrepreneurs are often much too casual about this. A partner not only needs to meet your talent/capital requirements they also must be compatible with your personality and share your values and goals. I would go so far as to say that it would be a good idea if they shared your politics. **S.J.**f

*The surest path to success is paved with uniqueness.

Having a truly unique product trumps everything else. If you think you have this ignore the naysayers, forget about the economy, don't worry about lack of sufficient capital, do it and do it quickly. **J.S.**f.

*Absent a unique idea/product you must have the best price and/or service.

This is the path taken by most entrepreneurs. It is what is referred to as sweat-equity. It's not as sexy as a unique product, but if you are able to make it work it can be just as rewarding. **F.s.j.**

APPENDIX: RODGER'S RESTAURANT RULES

The following is for all those poor souls who wish to make the a la carte restaurant their self- employment destination.

*Don't rent

Unless you're in a large city, restaurants with their low profit margins, don't generate enough bottom line for the amount of hard work required. Your payout comes when you sell. The sale price will be greatly increased if you own the building and property.

*Don't over-pay.

A restaurant with the building and adequate parking should fetch about one times gross annual sales, or if you aren't interested in their business, the appraised value of the land and building plus the going price of a local liquor license. Which leads to…

*Try to buy a place that has a liquor license.

A liquor license, in addition to its appeal to your potential customers, is usually limited by state or local regulations. This limits your possible competition.

*Do a thorough demographic study.

You must get a handle on the make-up of the population within ten miles of the place that you're interested in. A business plan that works in one locale may be a dismal failure in another.

*Don't buy a place with a septic system.

Ok, this one's not an absolute, but be aware that septic systems and commercial dishwashers are not an ideal match.

*Try to buy a restaurant that has most of the parking in back

This may sound a little weird, but empty parking lots tend to stay empty, full lots tend to get even fuller. People like to patronize busy places. It's tough to get the first few patrons to pull into an empty lot that is visible from the road. Which leads to…

*Have your employees' park in the front.

If your lot is visible from the road this makes it easier to get those first few customers in.

*Try to buy a place that has a separate banquet area.

A space that holds fifty plus would be nice. Private parties are more profitable that a la carte dining and provide revenue during slow times.

*Don't expect to score financing with anyone but the seller.

Banks hate restaurants. 29% down with the balance over 10 to 15 years at two points over prime is reasonable when the seller is holding paper. You might ask your broker about the possibility of S.B.A. financing.

*Brokers are a mixed bag.

They are expensive- 6 to 10% commissions are the rule and the seller will increase his price accordingly. This can add a lot to the purchase price. They will show you a lot of properties that, if they're good, fit your parameters. They can be very knowledgeable, and find you some financing. They can also be knuckle heads and waste your time Ask your local restaurant association for recommendations.

*Have your chef look at the kitchen.

Remodeling the kitchen can be **very** expensive.

*Implement a fair tipping policy.

Danny Meyer is a titan of the restaurant industry, and he recently banned tipping at all of his fine dining establishments. The reason? People who worked "front of the house" (waiters, waitresses, bartenders) were making more from tips than "back of the house" employees were making in salary. So he banned tipping, raised menu prices (a lot), and made the pay more equitable.

Now the tipping system as it exists in this country is not perfect. There are skinflint customers who will tip 10% regardless of how good the service is, and generous souls who will tip arrogant, lazy waiters 25%, but in the vast majority of cases wait staff will receive compensation based on their performance. This is the reason that you'll never get "Have a nice day" instead of "Thank you" from your server. Tipping should be extended to other parts of retail rather than being eliminated!

The solution to the income disparity problem lies in a good house tipping policy. Waiters in most restaurants "tip out" at the end of a shift, giving a portion of their tips to employees that helped them earn it. This may involve 5% to 10% to the bus staff and 10% to 15% to the bartenders. How about another 10% to 15% to the kitchen staff? This would not only make pay more equitable at your place, but give your kitchen staff an incentive to pick up their game on busy nights.

Danny, you're a hell of a restaurateur and I loved you book , but on this one you're dead wrong.

Mr. Meyer is a Scrooge, I believe, albeit with a nice dollop of the other two types. I'm guessing 45% Scrooge, 30% Fezziwig, and 25% Jorkin. He sees his employees as helpmates in the building of his financial fortune. I, as a strong Fezziwig, see employees as students eager to be taught the proper way (my way) to satisfy the customer. A strong Jorkin sees her employees as knights-errant willing and able to be led in her quest to change the world.

They are all three types, special.

God bless the capitalists.

Rodger Cornell currently resides with his wife in Allamuchy, New Jersey.

He can be contacted via his email at rkcornell77@gmail.com

25633881R00065

Printed in Great Britain
by Amazon